This book is dedicated to my mother Joan

Robertson.

Mom, I love you.

And to Rose of course, my one and only.

TABLE OF CONTENTS

HOW TO START YOUR OWN SUCCESSFUL INSURANCE AGENCY AND MAKE A FAMILY BUSINESS WORK

By Scott Robertson, CPCU

I would like to teach you how and inspire you to start and operate your own successful insurance agency. I started my own nine years ago after working as a producer in agencies for over a decade. I call this my apprenticeship period. My apprenticeship began in 1992 when I began as a business sales rep for Liberty Mutual and ended after a two year partnership in a small agency ended without me having the opportunity to buy the agency from the owner. As with many other business owners, I did not glide easily into agency ownership. I was rudely shoved by an unsuccessful partnership and circumstances out of that middle world state of ambitious employee to fledgling agency owner.

It did not seem like the right time; it never does. Opportunity does not knock when you are ready, it catches you unawares and you have to just try it. Or you can spend the rest of your life wondering what it would have been like to go out on your own and be your own boss.

There are steps you have to go through before you go out on your own. First, you have to apprentice with other agencies and or insurers in order to learn your craft. The more variety the better. For example I was a business sales rep for a mutual insurer, a large regional agency, a small local agency and a global broker. All these experiences gave me different valuable perspectives on different insurance environments. You will compete with all of these types of brokers so it is imperative you learn about them, the better from the inside where you get a much more detailed realistic experience.

Second, you have to educate yourself in insurance coverages. You want the other agents you compete with to say of you, "You know your coverages." How to educate yourself? First, the experience of working daily in the insurance world selling policies is a great starter. But this learning curve can flatten out as you become ingrained in your daily routine. Also, people tend to gravitate to those fields in which they have successfully sold insurance in the past. So someone who gets real estate agent clients will continue to sell to real estate agents. Which is great and can open up group and association insurance opportunities in the future. But from an experience perspective, it can lead to a narrowing of focus. One of the best educational tools is the accreditation program, such as the CPCU or ARM programs. You have to invest your time in reading the books. Plus to get credit you have to take and pass the national exams at a testing center. By mixing your effort and money in the pursuit of insurance and insurance related knowledge, your knowledge will grow. You will become a more well rounded agent.

Third, save money. You will need at least 3 months of personal living expenses plus start up costs and operating expenses when you start your own agency. You can estimate your personal living expenses by what you have spent in the past. But start up costs and operating costs are based on projections, and you need to be as accurate as possible. Which brings me to the fourth thing you need to do before starting your own agency.

Write a business plan. You can buy business plan template software which allows you to worry about content rather than form. Or you can write your own. Begin with a summary paragraph of your history, qualifications, customer base and services you will offer. Then you go into detail on your customers, carriers you will represent, staffing and revenue and expense projections. Be realistic about expenses and revenues. In my first year, my expenses were double my projections while my revenues were half. But don't undercut yourself either. One of the applications of your business plan is in the financing of your start up business. The first thing a bank will ask you for is your business plan. It's better to have it ready than to have to play catch up and formulate one on deadline. Another use of your business plan is as a guide for that critical first year. You should refer to it if you feel uncertain about the way your business is going. I applied for and was accepted for a small business loan of $50,000. I declined it because of the onerous reporting requirements of the program. I would have had to show receipts and fill out a report detailing every single expense for the agency using those funds. It would have cost me more time and trouble than it was worth when I could just take a second mortgage on the house at a slightly higher interest rate. The confidence of getting the first loan I applied for as a business owner was worth going through the loan exercise, more important than the money itself. And the experience of doing a business plan was useful.

Finally, keep a list of your best clients and be prepared to contact them for support, future business and advice. As a commercial lines broker many of my clients were invaluable sources of advice. They had gone through exactly the same process I had, working for other businesses in sales or operations and then going out on their own. In my case, I apprenticed with a small agency owner with an agreement to buy his book of business. When this didn't work out, I found myself out on the street and was devastated. My life suffered. My marriage suffered. I got paranoid that everyone was out to get me. They weren't; one extremely bad situation colored my perception of the world. I told my story to a number of my clients and one out of two told me they had had the same experience with an unsuccessful apprenticeship before they finally opened their own business!

CHAPTER 1: GET LICENSED

The requirement that agencies must be licensed by each state's department of insurance before they can transact insurance business is beneficial to established agents and to the public. It ensures that agents selling insurance have some basic knowledge of the complex products they are offering to the public which in general knows virtually nothing about insurance. Inept agents give the whole industry a black eye so public confidence in agents gained by license helps the industry as a whole. Also, licensing is a barrier to entry in the business of selling insurance. This keeps the casual unserious competitor out of the business. On the negative side, getting licensed is an arduous process. It begins with taking at least a week of classes in insurance culminating in the insurance licensing exam. You have to pass the exam to get your license. When I first took my exam I was fresh out of college and I was pretty confident that I didn't need to review the material much. I failed it the first time much to my embarrassment. I thought I was a bad ass in the classroom. Well like life you get out of insurance what you put into it. Being first exposed to insurance is entering a completely different world with a language of its own. Many of the forms haven't substantially changed since the policies were first drafted at Lloyds in the 16th century to cover wine barrels making their way across a perilous ocean. It is not difficult but insurance is an arcane subject which must be taken on seriously not treated lightly. I swaggered into my insurance exam and limped out with my tail between my legs. Do what I didn't do the first time, take the exam review course and take the test seriously. I took the review course and scored a 96 on the test. It just takes effort and a willingness to immerse yourself in the new terms and way of looking at the world as rife with exposures and how to treat those exposures.

CHAPTER 2: PROCEDURES TO GET SET UP

So you're licensed and ready to blast out on your own. There are some nuts and bolts things you have to do before you are street legal to sell your first policy. The first thing is to make sure you have the correct insurance license and endorsements on that license. The name on your license and fictitious business name (dba): must match the name of your organization. In California for instance if you are a sole proprietor the name of your agency can be your name individually. If you have an individual agent/broker license and you are a sole proprietor without a dba, you are ready to go. However many agents have a business name they want to hold out to the public and to do that you must endorse the DBA: on your agent/broker license. This requirement can delay the launch of your business so plan ahead and give yourself plenty of time to correctly license your agency. When the department of insurance is busy it can take up to 6 weeks to get your license endorsed. Be careful about this step. When your license gets endorsed it goes on your state's department of insurance website. If you are still working for another agency and they monitor your license or happen to be checking your license, your DBA: will be visible to them. This will telegraph your plans to the agency if you weren't going to tell them your plans until you were out on your own. So it can be a double bind. If you start too early to get your license endorsed you run the risk of your present employer seeing your new business name emblazoned across the internet. If you wait until you have resigned and are out on your own you could delay the startup of your business. Every moment counts when you go out on your own in a competitive situation with your former employer. You need to hit the ground running and write or broker your business as soon as possible.

You are going to be under a lot of pressure to get the commission coming in, but don't cut corners and write business before you are properly licensed. Do it the legal way. Your competition will be watching you closely for slip ups and this could be a big one. They could turn you into the department of insurance for a code violation if you are writing business without the correct license. This will slow you up considerably as you apply for appointments with carriers or try to run with a cluster. One of the first things prospective carriers and agency groups ask is if you have any E&O's

or insurance code violations, which includes proceedings investigating such violations. You have to write business and put food on the table, but you will be doing yourself a long term disservice if you don't properly license yourself. Most licensing forms are available online so the important thing is to fill them out and get them in correctly. If they are not correct the department will kick them back to you marked up in red. Avoid this waste of precious time and do the forms right the first time. Call the DOI if you have questions.

Get a broker bond if your state requires it. This is mandatory in California and is another often overlooked requirement that slows up prospective agency owners. Go online and order it or go through another agent if you are not familiar with bond placements. The bond is cheap in terms of premium and is designed to compensate your customer if you abscond with their money much like a contractor's license bond. Also, buy a business license in your town if they require it and join the chamber of commerce. Word to the wise this will trigger a visit by the fire department to inspect your premises for fire protection. With clerical occupancies they seem to look for exposed extension cords the most. Even though you are an office and present less of a fire exposure than say a manufacturing entity, the fire department will still send someone out. Have a fire extinguisher in your office and working smoke detectors as well. If you are in a large building, the fire department inspector will most likely be familiar with your location and the inspection shouldn't take too long. In any event don't be surprised if they come calling after you apply for a business license.

It sounds ridiculous but remember to do just as good a job with your own agency's risk management and insurance program as you devote to others. It is easy to overlook your own program when you do it for a living . Shop for health insurance, workers' compensation, general liability, property, crime, errors & omissions, auto, umbrella liability, disability coverage and other coverages you may need to protect yourself, your employees, your family and your organization. You will have plenty of time to tweak your coverages over time, but it will save you effort to start with a good foundation of coverage for your agency. And as mentioned you will not be appointed with carriers without errors and omissions insurance. Likewise your license will not go through without the proper bonding if your state requires it.

CHAPTER 3: PAY YOUR DUES

To write business you need markets. Without companies with which to place insurance you are a consultant only. I have found that it is more rewarding both intellectually and financially to place insurance as an agent or broker. Some agents have found a niche as a professional insurance buyer for commercial clients. But unless you are in a major metropolitan area this is not a feasible option. Smaller clients need an agent to transact and service their insurance business throughout the year and not just a professional insurance buyer for a one time purchase of their insurance package.

To learn the markets you need to work at an agency or for a direct writer. How long? It depends on how much time you will need to build your book of business and establish contacts on both sides of the table of the insurance transaction, that is with the buyer of the coverage and the insurance company providing the coverage. A client told me that after I went out on my own I would regret that I did not do it 2 years sooner. This was not the case for me. I needed all of the ten years I apprenticed at different sized agencies before I was ready. But once I was ready I never looked back.

Part of paying your dues is having the courage to continue on your path towards agency ownership. You are handicapping yourself unnecessarily if you don't bear your ultimate objective of agency ownership in mind. For instance, if you get too comfortable working for someone else, you might sign a non compete agreement in a moment of weakness or inattention. Signing this agreement could get you in legal trouble later on and tie you up in court while you should be producing insurance. Don't sign a non compete agreement. If an agency principal asks you why you won't sign you should be truthful and tell them you are keeping your options open. You are happy but the markets could change and you don't want to get tied up.

There are many agency opportunities out there. It seems that every agency is looking for producers. What is the loss to them if it doesn't work out? The agency hires a producer, has them sign an ironclad non compete agreement and puts them to work cold calling. Or the agency has a professional phone solicitor who makes appointments. Nothing is free and usually there is some deduction of the producer's commission if the lead is generated by an agency paid phone solicitor. If it does not work out with the agent, the agency depending on how cold blooded they are fires the agent and keeps the business that was produced. Many times the ones doing the offering are slick producers themselves blowing smoke in your face. Do not be distracted by these offers. Over the years I have had many many such offers. Maybe a couple of them were fair and might have had legs, but most were better for the agency. So how do you keep your soul in a cutthroat industry in which you have a hidden agenda? You work as hard as you can for the agency, building your contacts in the process. Never lie to the agency about your long term goals. Most successful agencies are desperate for an entrepreneurial agent who makes things happen and treats their agency as if it were their business. The best agencies will try to make it worth your while to stay. Obviously you have resisted this sedentary temptation if you are reading this.

Keep your eyes open when you are in an agency for pitfalls as well as opportunities. Do not sign overly restrictive contracts that you will regret in the future when you are ready to open your own agency. Get to know underwriters at companies. Marketing people can be good contacts as well, but underwriters are the ones who will have direct knowledge of the type and quality of business and the all important loss ratio of your book.

A tactic used by agencies to keep the agent focused on selling is to have CSR's do all the day to day activities on the customers' files. Do not be lulled into a sense that selling is all you have to do and others can do the rest. Do your own certificates, submit your own claims, go out on loss control appointments, review billing. In short, experience all aspects of agency operations. You won't have a clue when you start your agency about the non selling facets of the business if you don't. Money is tight when you start out and you will most likely not have the working capital to hire your own customer service rep much less a loss control rep. You will have to do it yourself, along with billing agency billed accounts yourself.

CHAPTER 4: EDUCATE YOURSELF

There are many ways to distinguish yourself from the competition. But one of the best ways to distinguish yourself and train yourself to own your agency is to get one or multiple designations. I went through the American Institute of Insurance's Chartered Property Casualty Underwriter designation program. In 2000 this meant taking 10 courses and passing 10 national examinations which were in blue book format. Now the designation can be earned by passing 8 national exams in multiple choice format which are taken on computer at a learning center. I hate to sound like the old coots who glory about their much harder lives than the current younger generation, but the essay and short answer exams I took to get my designation seem a lot harder than today's exams. But in the end, who cares.

The point of getting these designations is refreshing and renewing your knowledge continuously and staying up on changes in the industry. Using CPCU, because I know it, you read about coverages you may never place in your career. I remember taking the life insurance part of the test. It helps to be a more well rounded agent to know a little bit about life insurance and financial services. What really helped was going over all of the coverages and exclusions of the property and general liability policies. I had more knowledge and became better at my job because of the added confidence which taking and passing the exams gave me. Also, having the designation can get you appointments with buyers familiar with insurance which you would not have gotten if you came in as Joe Agent. The designation can open doors for you to sell more insurance by giving you instant credibility as someone who knows about what they are selling.

I would not necessarily put the CPCU program over the CIC program, both are very good programs. However, if you choose a program that is less than rigorous or which has open book exams, it is too tempting not to give it your full attention. If you need the discipline of a classroom to force yourself to study and assimilate the material, then get a study group or take a formalized class. CPCU yields results with both learning methods.

Read the books and take the tests. I remember a teacher of mine said there are two types of homework doers. One does it in their room with the door closed, free of all outside noises and distractions. The other does their homework on the kitchen table. However you learn take the courses seriously and apply them to your job. Education is another factor that will help you be ready to launch your own agency successfully.

Another way to educate yourself is to befriend other agents and people in your industry. This means staying on good terms with your competition. Often your competitors have information about which carriers or markets are writing which type of business most competitively. Compete but don't burn bridges with your companies as well. Companies go in and out of writing certain classes of business. Sometimes one company will be the hot company writing a particular class of business. Those are the times you need those companies. If you have consistently sent a company subpar business with high loss ratios or adverse characteristics, you will most likely be turned down when you try to get an appointment with the company. Or if you have an appointment, your apps will go to the bottom of the stack on the desk of the underwriter trainee you get.

CHAPTER 5: SAVE MONEY

It is hard to save money when you have expenses such as college loans, rent on an apartment, an engagement ring, a wedding, a baby on the way, and clients to take to lunch. However you need to establish your credit early on so that when you go out on your own, you have a credit line. You will need to tap this credit line to pay your living, startup, and office expenses for a few months until commission checks begin to arrive with predictability. Predictability of income is very difficult for several reasons. One, you can't predict the market. If it's a soft market of decreasing rates and increasing capacity, your commission income will be reduced. You don't know which clients are coming with you. You will be surprised by those who stick with you and unfortunately those who don't. It is difficult to time the commission stream of income. Carriers generally pay you the month after they are paid by the insured so there is always a 2-3 month gap in a policy renewing and you getting paid.

So how much money should you have when starting your agency? Enough to pay your living and office expenses for at least 3 months. So I would have at least 3 months of net pay saved up for such items as a rent deposit, subscriptions to trade magazines, pens, paper and other incidentals. The long term assets you will need to invest in such as an agency management system, desks and computers can be put on a credit card or a second mortgage on the house. If you have applied for a small business loan, the bank will require a detailed list of exactly how you will be spending the loaned money, to be backed up by receipts of the actual expenditures. Remember that when you get commission you need to subtract a percentage that will go to Uncle Sam for taxes. No longer will you be getting a paycheck from an employer with all of the withholding tax calculations performed for you. It is up to you to make sure you have enough to pay your taxes at the end of the year. After you have been up and running a while you will start paying your taxes on a quarterly estimated basis. This is a drain on your resources but it does help you from owing a large sum at the end of the year.

Whatever you think that 3 month number of necessary funds is, double it. It takes a lot of cash to start your own agency, more than you think while you are in the planning stage. The unexpected expenses get you. At the beginning, I was financing my wife's college education. Unexpectedly, the tuition fees virtually doubled overnight and the cost of textbooks seemed to go up as she progressed in her studies. I had to find that extra money for my home life.

This keeps many people from starting their own business: The fear that spouses and families will not tolerate the decrease in income. I had the same fear. Talk to your spouse, communicate that this is something you are meant to do or have always wanted to do and that it will lead to greater resources for your family and fulfillment for you. You will be surprised at how supportive your spouse will be if your heart is in your dreams as the Disney song goes. The same goes for your kids. How can you coach them to reach for the stars and follow their dreams when you won't? There is no guarantee you will succeed, but you will always wonder if you don't try.

CHAPTER 6: HAVE A PLAN

Having a plan means writing a business plan. I know you have it in your head the trajectory of your efforts: Commit to the business, rent space, buy/lease office equipment, contact your customers and get selling!

But doing this is like arriving at the ocean. All you want to do is get to the beach and swim. Likewise as a new business owner all you want to do is sell sell sell with unlimited potential. No splits with the agency owners, you keep what you sell. But know that ignoring the details of starting your business will still be around even if you ignore them. One of the most important things to do is write a business plan. Myriad business plan software exists. You can spend a lot of money or no money if you want to do it on your own. The important thing is a business plan should meet your needs not someone else's, though it might serve both purposes of a road map for you and a requirement for a small business loan.

A business plan requires you to think through several aspects of your business that your mental overview lacks. For example, will you be a sole proprietor? Incorporate? Hire an employee? How many customers do you think will move their business to you? What kind of agency management system will you use? How much will that cost? How will you pay for it? How about the name of your business...The many elements of having a business and the costs you may miss such as the cost of a broker bond find their way onto paper and into the light of a business plan.

CHAPTER 7: WORK YOUR CONTACTS

Networking comes easily to many salespeople, not so easy to some. As salespeople we are expected to be outgoing, gregarious and hale fellow well met types who can work a room of strangers. We are expected to be able to establish rapport with others quickly. The knock on these types of people who establish friendships too easily is that the bonds are skin deep, based on money and in general are superficial. So it doesn't hurt to be a little reserved as you establish a working relationship. You want clients for life not a quick score and then move on to the next customer. There is no perfect sales type. There is a place for taciturn saturnine salespeople. There is a place for people who are not gregarious or who are terrified of a roomful of people they are expected to meet and greet. This is because there are all sorts of personality types of customers. Not all insurance buyers appreciate backslappers. In fact, most of the business insurance buyers are in finance and are CFO's or accountaints and are generally more reserved personality types. So never let anyone tell you you don't have the personality for sales. If you want to do it, you can, and you can find customers who reflect your personality and whose personality you reflect. I remember someone I came across in the insurance world who had an extremely overbearing personality. He acted like the stereotypical bully on the playground, using intimidation to make his points and was big and not too bright just like the stereotype. However, his family had money and he was able to get in doors that way. Also, he was a snob. He belonged to a country club and looked down on all of us in the office as life forms lesser than he. He once told me that his country club didn't allow tank tops when I asked about the possibility of me golfing there with my family members. What amazed me is this schmuck had plenty of clients and a relatively high position. True, he lost a lot once they got to know him and found him to be even more obnoxious than he came across initially. But he had a decent sized book of business. My point here is that there are a lot of stupid, elitist, schmucks who buy insurance and don't belong in their positions either. Don't let your personality type ever limit you from sales.

You can make contacts anywhere sometimes where you least expect. For instance, I got my start in insurance as a result of being in my college friend's wedding. His wife told me about a business insurance sales representative opening at Liberty Mutual. I had never considered insurance or risk management as a career, but I applied for and accepted the job Liberty offered. While at the wedding I made contact with a gentleman involved in an insurance networking organization. He turned out to be a great contact I stayed in touch with; he put me in touch with my next employer after Liberty Mutual. The point is, stay attuned to your surroundings, always be on the lookout for contacts.

When I started out I got the local Chamber of Commerce directory and called every single name in the book. This was before elaborate voice mail. Nearly every caller rejected me, some politely while others found it to be their job in life to humiliate me. They would tell me to find another business. Or they would hang up in my face. Another one told me never ever and I mean never to call again. Turns out his wife actually ran the business while he answered phones. I would go home with my head hanging down, thinking I couldn't do this job because it was too hard. Instead of coddling me my newlywed wife gave me a lesson in tough love. She told me to get used to rejection and that if I couldn't take it, I wouldn't last in this business. You know what, she was right. Her bracing words bucked me up and I kept at it. That's the important lesson, to stick to what you are doing. Sure you can improve your technique but you have to continue working. Be prepared for tough tough times but know that these are necessary to reach your objective of agency ownership.

Use humiliating treatment and insulting comments by others when you are starting out as fuel for your future achievement. Remember this feeling in order to overcome the fear of going out on your own.

Chapter 8: STRUGGLE

The saying about it being darkest before dawn has to apply to insurance agents. That's what I thought when I had gone from working as a producer for a mega broker to a so called partnership with a small local agent. My plan which I communicated to the agency owner was to apprentice with him for a couple of years, make sure it was a fit, and then buy the agency from him when he retired. What I thought was genuine agreement was in fact a sales job to get me to bring my book to his small agency. So I burned and learned as they say. However, I was devastated emotionally. Just two years before I had taken a leap of faith and trusted the word of this longtime agent and moved my accounts through the tedious process of Broker of Record letters which each client had to sign. And I had to compete with my former employer who wanted to keep my accounts. In order for my clients to transfer their business to my new agency I had to make the case effectively that I was taking a step forward and this was a safe secure place for their business. So two years later I was faced with going to these same customers and telling them I was changing course again. It wouldn't have worked if I was going to work for another agency.

The reason it worked was my explanation was backed by reality that the inevitable had occurred. I was now, finally, going to open my own agency. Because most of my clients had followed exactly the same path, going from employee to apprentice to business owner, I was able to transfer my accounts. The cost was enormous. It took a huge toll on my life to have to go through another job move. Many, many business owners I spoke with experienced the same process of apprenticeship and then betrayal by owners who really just wanted someone to do all the work while they profited from it. The carrot of business ownership they dangled in front of our eyes proved illusory in many cases.

However, the ultimate benefit of this extremely bitter experience was the birth of my agency. In the disorder and uncertainty of those times I found the catalyst to open my business. It took this darkness for me to finally go to the light and go out on my own. I needed a very strong push and I got it. I was broke and penniless and the agent was threatening to steal all my accounts and sue me, the same person who had courted me and shamelessly flattered me, calling me the best insurance agent in Monterey County. This was a very strange jarring experience, but one that I used to my advantage. Struggle can be hard and bitter and disillusioning but there is nothing like it to toughen you up and galvanize you to action. Take defeat and misfortune as lessons and get busy to turn things around.

So what happens when another agency has your business written under their producer code? This means they get the commissions on your business and profit sharing. To get it out from under them you need to have your client sign a letter appointing your agency as broker of record. You must have an appointment with the carrier in order for the broker transition to take place. You can do the letter yourself by putting the client's letterhead on top and ghost writing the body of the letter signaling their intention to transfer their insurance to you. An officer of the corporation or the owner must sign the letter. But the easier you make it for your client to sign their business over to you, the more likely you are to succeed in getting that letter. Once you send in the signed broker of record letter the other agent has 10 days to get a rescinding letter.

You should tell your client that they will probably hear from the other agent after you send this letter to the carrier. I had a client who was peeved with me that I did not tell him the other agent would be pestering him. He thought the letter put him on a "do not call" list from the other agent which is not the case. Each carrier is slightly different in what they require re: the format and timing of these letters so read your agency guidelines or talk to your underwriter or marketing rep so you don't have to redo the letter. Also, some carriers won't accept BOR's unless they are within 60 days of your client's renewal date. Do not fall into the trap of overpromising and underdelivering by telling your client they can transfer their business to you and it doesn't happen because of the carrier requirements of which you were ignorant.

One of the greatest lessons I took from this struggle of being beaten down to nothing and having to rebuild was the closeness it created with my loving wife. In my struggle i did not include my wife at first. I took it all on my shoulders as if it were my burden to bear alone. This was selfish of me and had disastrous results. After my experience with my previous business partner I became distrustful of others. My wife and I came very close to splitting because of all the stress in our lives and on our marriage. But we fought hard for our marriage, and these tough times brought us closer together.

After my wife got her 4 year college degree we began to work together. My wife made an agreement with me to receive her bachelor's degree before she would come to work in the agency. She never wanted to have a job in the business just because of her position as the wife. She is a very strong proud person who took her job and made herself indispensable to the business. And that meant scrubbing toilets, filing a lot of paperwork, answering phones and licking envelopes. We have never looked back. We work together very well. We both do what it takes to make our agency successful whether that is taking out the garbage or working on a weekend or holiday to help out a client with a claim. My point is it took my marriage going to the very brink of oblivion to recreate itself and grow into a loving relationship. Don't let it get that far. Keep your partner involved in what you are doing and share with them what you are experiencing. I kept my bitterness to myself and closed myself off from my wife and it almost killed us.

Another related lesson from my agency's painful beginnings was that through that pain I learned to value my own business that much more than if it had been easy. I can't tell you how I dreaded going to each of my clients and asking them to sign the broker of record letters two years after I had asked them to do the same. I told them 2 years previously that I had found a better situation for me and for them and most had believed in me and transferred their account to a smaller agency they had never heard of before. Now I was pitching the same idea to them but when the previous "great situation for us both" was still fresh in their minds.

With most, honesty worked. I told them I was making this move to truly open my own agency after a bad experience which I mistakenly thought would lead to my agency ownership. I found that many shared my experience of apprenticing without getting the opportunity to buy the business. Most of my clients started their own businesses just this way and identified with my situation. So the final lesson of this ugly dreadful time is to tell the truth and sell to clients you identify with and who identify with you. Part of using the struggle as fuel to launch your own agency is to use problems, setbacks and humiliations to propel you to bigger and better things. That means don't let anything get you down permanently. Setbacks like losing clients and getting yelled at for a stupid move really sting, I don't deny that. But the smart ones don't make the same mistake twice. And there is no lesson quite as strong as pain to etch itself in your memory.

CHAPTER 9: WORKING WITH FAMILY

My agency evolved from something I started and worked in by myself for 3 years. My wife began working in the agency after she earned her Bachelor of Arts degree in 2003. My agency transformed into our agency. A year later the business evolved again. We rented an office where my wife grew up in the growing location of Selma, CA. Selma is the number one grower of raisins in the country. We wanted to turn our agency into the number one provider of insurance coverage and service. My commercial lines clients were constantly asking us to do their personal lines in addition to their commercial insurance. After hearing this for so long my wife and I finally decided to start offering personal lines rather than referring it to other agents. Customers like to keep their Property & Casualty insurance under one roof and like to make one call for their insurance needs rather than having to remember a different phone number for each type of insurance they carry.

One of the things we needed to do to succeed in Selma was to get a sales rep there. My commercial book of business was mostly in Salinas and so we needed someone working in that office. After a lot of discussion and one amazing significant event, Rose's sister decided to join us as our personal lines manager. She was well qualified, having 20 years of personal lines sales experience at the well respected direct writer Liberty Mutual.

Sarah went back and forth on coming to work with us. She was comfortable and had seniority at Liberty Mutual. She had no idea what commissions she could earn on her own with us. One Sunday when she and her husband were visiting us in Salinas, we went to church and something amazing occurred. The weekend she was going to make her decision whether to join us or stay at Liberty Mutual, the priest's homily was about how good it is to take a risk and try something new and wonderful. He seemed to be pointing his finger at her as he recommended people to take a chance to improve yourself. The priest turned out to be a dear friend who accompanied us to Hawaii twice as our friend, spiritual guide and golfing buddy. Father Bob Murrin also had worked as an executive for many years in a life insurance company before taking his orders.

So it was a nearly miraculous confluence of events that finally blessed Sarah's decision to work with us. Sarah took a leap of faith to come with us. True, we had shown a positive profitable track record for this business the previous 3 years. And it was manifestly worth Sarah's while to come with us. Working with us meant no commute compared with a 30 minute commute each way every day to Liberty Mutual. Control over her book of business and ownership of her percentage of her book. The quality of life was squarely in favor of coming with us. The money was better the other way. However, when you run into a problem like this where one factor is positive and the other is negative, work it out. We could have walked away and never opened an office in Rose's home town. But we were committed to find a way to make it work.

Money is always a huge factor in anyone's decision to get a job. But it makes sense to relate money to broader concepts of value. That's what we did with Sarah. She couldn't have gone on commission at first since she was not bringing a book of business with her. You might be scratching your head and wondering if I was crazy to bring someone over with no book of business and to defray her salary and benefits. Well, this is where faith on both sides came in. Sarah agreed to take lower pay and I agreed to pay her while she was building her book. My point in this is to relate money and commute and job security to value. Money is part of value but value far transcends money. That's how we were able to convince Sarah to come work with us.

After we crossed this milestone, the key was to make it work in the business. Family business makes heroes of us all. My wife Rose and her sister Sarah felt each other out for months, trying on this new relationship of coworkers. One of the differences between family and work is how you argue. There have to be lines drawn in business arguments so that the inevitable conflicts don't resemble tiffs over the Thanksgiving holiday table. You have to build back a layer of formality at work so the easy family relationship does not get in the way of work being done. In other words, make ground rules like no kids if they are getting in the way, or limit personal phone calls if they become excessive. It is critical that you the owner follow the rules you prescribe for others. Otherwise, you are guaranteed to build resentments which will gradually start as grumbles and whispers and then manifest themselves in an avalanche of anger and bitterness.

One of these cataclysmic events happened at my mother in law's breakfast table when my sister in law yelled at my wife, "I hate you." She then stormed out, sobbing. The lines between sister and boss and employee became blurred. They call each other nickhames as family members do but at work the same informal practices do not apply. This episode highlights the importance of limiting discussion about work at family get togethers. I am not going to be so naïve as to say there can be no talk about business. It is inevitable that there be some talk about work which consumes at least 40 hours of everyone's life a week. Word to the wise though, do not let it be the only thing you talk about. It will alienate the family members who do not work in the business to have to listen to talk about the business. It will cause the business to become stale when it's the only topic on the table and breed resentment and burn out.

Here are a couple of things to remember when you have family members who are working in your business. If they are bringing revenue in, get a "key employee" life insurance policy on them. You decide on the limit but a good rule of thumb in selecting the limit would be the commission income attributable to the family member for however long it would take to find another employee to perform their duties. You can modify the limit by several factors such as the cost to conduct an agent search and the salary to hire the new employee.

Another thing to remember for your agency is to make it as much like a business as possible. It is too tempting to structure the business like you would put together a family touch football game. Be informal yes and cut a lot of slack to everyone such as long lunches and days off or bringing babies into work. But make sure everyone meets the expectations you have for them. If your brother in law or brother is your partner or employee make sure you set goals and demand accountability. Let's face it, firing a family member is not going to happen; it would devastate the family and probably cause irreparable damage to family relationships. But you can tie pay to performance and you can reassign jobs if someone is not getting it done. If your brother comes to work for you as a sales rep because he doesn't want to work in the outside 9-5 world anymore, make sure you have an exit strategy to save face for both of you if it doesn't work out. You can do this without being a jerk.

With all this inevitable drama playing out as work and family roles diverge, find a way to make it work. There will be lots of problems. We have all come to the conclusion that we are all part of the problem in our own ways and part of the solution too. Because we talk about our issues we work on them. They are still there and will always be a part of family and business, but we have resolved to make it work and so can you in your family business.

CHAPTER 10: SETTING SALARIES AND HANDLING FINANCIAL INFORMATION

In insurance compensation for salespeople is pretty straightforward. Pay is based on a percentage of the commission they earn. How to pay that commission can be tricky. Do you pay the entire commission up front or do you pay as it is earned. The answer depends on whether you are paying a draw or straight commission. And this in turn depends on how experienced the agent is.

In the case of my sister in law, she came with us from Liberty Mutual who had a strict non piracy agreement.

Sarah had to rebuild her book of business from no accounts. So to be fair we negotiated a salary to start for a period of 4 years until she could write enough accounts to go on commission. If you have a new agent you have to pay them up front and hope they will make it up on the back end when they gain experience. Some pay new agents a draw, a salary taken against the promise of future commissions, but it would be very awkward to charge them back for commission if they make less than the draw amount. Also, once that draw is spent, memories become short, and it gets increasingly more difficult to collect back commission. If they don't make the draw they are not working out and that is already a bad situation. It is better just to pay them for a trial period. If it doesn't work out then it is better that you cut your ties with the agent or if it's family, you need to reassign them to support so they don't continue to cost you money.

An agent with an existing book of business can be paid on a straight commission basis. Sometimes the book is multiplied by the commission percentage the agent is getting and paid out over 26 pay periods. The agent can lose out if they write more business during the year than their percentage of commission figured at the beginning of the salary year. But the overriding goal is for fairness to you and your producer. If the commission plans are sloped too much in one's favor, the other will be pissed off and will resent the success of the other. The feeling of being taken advantage of is horrible. It kept me up at night, stewing in an impotent rage. Don't do that to yourself if you are the owner by giving away the store. And don't do it to someone else who needs a break in the business and more than that needs incentive and the feeling of working for an organization who values and needs their contribution. Give your producers partial ownership of the book of business they originate and produce. Make it a win win so that you will be friends forever even if the other person leaves the agency or the business.

One way to balance the security of a salary, which people like, with the incentive to produce is a base salary plus commission. The base is a percentage of the agent's book and the commission is based on new business production during the year.

What about chargebacks for lost business and errors and omissions claims and other thorny issues? The base salary should stay the same for the year and should be adjusted for lost business at the beginning of the next year. That means the base doesn't get adjusted during the year. If the producer nets a big one, the incentives for commission on new business will be the reward for production.

Another thorny issue occurs if the agent gets an Errors and Omissions claim he or she should pay the deductible. If there are multiple claims you should find yourself another producer. Everybody can get tagged with an E&O given our litigious society, but more than one could indicate a pattern which will cost you in reputation and dollars in terms of the inevitable increase in E&O premium on renewal depending on the severity and circumstances of the claim. Underwriters plug in loss amounts, including defense expenses since this is professional liability, and this increases the expected loss factor and consequently the premium.

CHAPTER 11: WHEN IS THE RIGHT TIME TO SELL OUT TO ANOTHER AGENCY AND IS THERE A RIGHT TIME?

As a fiercely independent agency owner I was struck by the irony of what happened after I first went out on my own. I received one job offer after the next as an insurance agency producer, more action than I ever got when I was working for someone else. Some of the offers were to sell my book and work as a producer on that book as well as producing new business. It was as if I had become irresistible forbidden fruit to other agencies which they had to have. Or more likely I had proved my bona fides as a genuine self starter, with the acumen and wherewithal to start my own agency and service my clients. I was not interested in their offers years ago and I am not interested today in selling my agency.

I had an agency owner offer to write me a check for the agency right there on the spot in my agency. I was in debt and my agency was just getting on its feet. I did think about it for at least a second. Who wouldn't, you're only human. Then I shook my head and remembered the situation I had just come from. Any amount of money was not worth the heartache and trouble of that experience. In the end, if you sell your book, it's theirs, not yours. Remember that part and the ramifications of working for someone else when agency owners dangle money in front of your nose in order to get you to sell your agency to them.

When I first started the agency in 2001 my friend and another insurance agent I had known and referred business to over the years allowed me to set up shop in a two room suite in his building near downtown. He didn't charge me rent for the first month but I made it up to him when I got on my feet. I don't like being in debt, and it was a point of professional pride to pay him back. It was almost as if paying him back for that month of rent was an indicator of my future success of my agency. My friend had been on his own for 10 years and had 4 employees in his business. He was always urging me to go on my own. I looked up to him as an entrepreneur, a true independent.

So I guess I was lulled into thinking that inertia would determine that he was never going to sell his book of business and that my wife and I could rent there forever. I don't think so. He told me a year before his move that he was entertaining an offer to become part of one of the largest insurance brokerages in the country and if he did I would have to move since I would be in competition with that firm. I did not think he was serious. He was. Two weeks before Christmas he emailed that he had signed a letter of intent to sell his book to them and merge his business with theirs. I guess I saw it coming. He did offer me to stay there and we remain dear friends today who don't compete with each other's accounts.

Did he do it at the right time? I know for him the deal made sense. If you are nearing retirement and need the proceeds from your book, that is the time to do it. But you can't wait until you are too old to sell because then the other party will have the leverage due to you needing to sell. Probably the best time to look for buyers is at least two years before you are ready to sell. You are going to have to live on the sale of your book so you need to negotiate from a position of strength, not weakness which waiting until the last minute will cause.

Determining when and to whom to sell comes down to three factors: 1) The time of your life and if you are ready to move on or retire 2) The condition of your book of business and the state of the market. 3) The credit worthiness and honor of the agency to which you are selling. Find someone you have worked with, respected and even competed with over the years. If you have had bad experiences with the agency while competing with them, if they were underhanded in how they tried to win or keep the business, then most likely they will try to take advantage of you during the sales and negotiation process.

If possible try to sell to an agency like yours. Selling to a big broker would be inconsistent with your agency over all the years. You left the large agency to give your clients a more personalized experience and to fulfill your dream of business ownership and you are abandoning your mission and clients for a couple of bucks? I have a better idea. Get a buy sell agreement in place with an agent or agency you have worked well with over time. If either one of you retires, becomes incapacitated or dies first, the other buys the agency from the estate. Tell your clients you have a succession plan in place. If you have saved your money over the years you should be able to choose the agency you sell to, not be chosen by someone else. To do that you need to invest your money wisely.

CHAPTER 12: WHEN YOU HAVE SOME MONEY LEFT OVER INVEST IT

When you start out, pay as little rent as possible. Some agents want to be in an affluent location and are willing to go into debt to have that location. If the location brings in enough commission to defray the rent, great, do it. But it has been my experience that the location is secondary to the agent's service level, skill and market knowledge. When you are young the client wants to see you a little hungry, not subsisting under a huge debt load of a large opulent office. Now when you reach a certain age, you will have to get better digs. Again, it has been my experience that clients expect you to do better the longer you are in business. If you have a crap office 20 years after you start your own agency it tells your clients that you haven't done well enough to afford better. That is troubling to clients and sends the wrong message.

So when you start, do it frugally with respect to your office digs. I bought and assembled my own desks, bookcases and chairs when I first opened my office. I saved money by keeping the office equipment simple and cheap. The same goes for my office. An insurance agent friend put me up in a modest 2 suite office in the building he owned. Not only did I get property/casualty referrals from him, I got a very good deal on rent. So I was able to save money on the rent, make money by writing his P&C insurance and make money by writing his P&C referrals. I also returned the favor by referring him quite a bit of health business from my own group of clients.

After you have been in your office a couple of years and have built your book of business up to pay your expenses with something left over for retirement and/or college funds for your kids, it is time to look for a building. This is where for me the family business aspect of my agency played a major role in my purchasing decision. We had opened our agency in the small town in which my wife grew up as I mentioned in a previous chapter. Next door fortuitously the building went up for sale. It was the building where the old JC Penney in town was located for 40 years. After 20 years of falling into disuse from occasional tenants, the building price was cheap. So my wife and sister in law and I decided to buy the building due to its price, location, good solid construction and name recognition.

This was a way to invest some of the money we had made over 5 years of owning and operating the agency. Also, we had enough space to rent it out to other office occupancies to help us with our mortgage payments. It is important that you buy a building when it is feasible for you. You can write off the interest on the loan as a tax deduction and write off the depreciation of the building every year. When you buy your building make sure you put it in your name individually and rent it back to your office. Remember your agency has to be a corporation or LLC to create a different entity with the entity that owns the building. This accomplishes two things. One, it takes your building out of the business' assets and so would not be included in a judgment against the business, whether bankruptcy or liability. Two, it makes sense from a tax savings point of view. The income to you as landlord is expense to the agency so the rental income is taxable income to the landlord but a tax deduction to the agency. I have insured many people over the years and most create an arms length distance between their business which occupies the building and their ownership of the building as landlord.

It is nice as the building owner to be able to buy the insurance and in effect take the commission as a discount on the gross premium. Most agents write the policies net of commission since it doesn't make sense to pay more premium and get the same amount back as commission. I find it fun to write my own agency's insurance. I put the health insurance with a buddy and a source of P&C leads so that my health insurance premium dollar works for me.

CHAPTER 13: RESEARCH MARKETS FOR YOUR BUSINESS

I am always paranoid about other agencies and their programs. Many agencies are niche players specializing in one or two classes of business. They put this business into associations with various carriers in return for a group discount with the carrier. The problem with this approach is risk management 101. Do not put all your eggs in one basket. If there is a problem with this class of business, your business is in jeopardy. Or if another agency decides to write this class of business and can do it more competitively than your market, you stand a chance of losing your entire book. For instance, I knew somebody in the business who had an agricultural group with a work comp carrier. After NAFTA flowers were grown and sold more cheaply in foreign countries which lead to closing of most of these flower growers. This person had gotten rich on this group and lazy in that he did no prospecting of other types of business. He did not go out of business but it took him a couple of years to replace the flower growers with other business. He lost that commission income and it impacted his way of living. He had to cold call, prospect and write the business. That takes time. You should be prospecting other types of business even if you have developed a niche group.

How do you get markets? As previously mentioned you can join a cluster or try to go it alone. If you are like me and only have enough premium to get appointments with one or two of the major companies, this limits your competitiveness in terms of marketing your prospects. Often the first question out of the mouth of a risk manager is what markets do you have? If you answer one market and your competitors have this market, why would the prospect get a quote from you? That will be the first thing the other agent says about you once he or she knows you're out there, that you are a good agent but that you are a one horse agent. Unless you bring some serious risk management skills or have an exclusive program for a class of business with a company (and as discussed in the preceding paragraph it can be precarious to write only one class of business), why would a busy business owner, CFO or risk manager give you a shot at their business if you don't have at least a couple of carriers.

So let's say you have a few insurance companies you represent either through a cluster, by yourself or through a wholesaler. Some companies will cut deals with wholesalers and they in turn will allow retailers to go through them for quotes. The wholesaler is either the gatekeeper, screening applications for the company or they are more of a managing general agent handling the underwriting, claims and loss control pieces for the company. Once you have a few companies in your stable and you call a prospect and give them a successful thumbnail sketch of your business, the next step is to secure the markets you will want to access to quote their business. You should immediately ask the prospect to assign you the insurance company or companies you want. Get it in writing signed by the prospect if you can. This presupposes that you have already thought about the type of business you are calling and which companies would be the most appropriate in terms of coverage and pricing to sell this type of risk. Getting the companies assigned to you is an aggressive first step by you toward writing this business. Don't be shocked if the submission is blocked. Often incumbent agents flood the markets at least 90 days before the renewal, blocking other agents from quoting with those companies. This is where the company assignment letter will come in handy.

How do you know what the carriers write? I get so many emails from companies that I do not have time to read them all. But you have to glance at them because that's where you get it in writing what the carriers are writing. Especially note the carrier's newsletters. Newsletters often have a section listing the types of accounts and premiums of business written that month. Also, you can ask your underwriters over the phone or at carrier meetings what they are writing. It saves underwriters time to get applications for classes of business they are writing and have a good shot at if they go to the trouble of rating, applying credits and finally issuing a quote. These days most quotes start on the website with the agency inputting the information and getting an online indication. Most of the time these indications that have to be referred to an underwriter for final approval before the company will issue the policy. Follow up information like loss runs or photos can also be required to complete the submission and firm up the quote. If you write smaller accounts in the $500 to $50,000 premium range, you can quote most of your own business using the company's web rater. It is a good idea to input the information yourself so you really learn the account. It is amazing how the information on a particular client will stick if you input the data yourself. So if an underwriter calls you for further information you will most likely be able to discuss it intelligently immediately rather than having to go to your file and call back the underwriter. The underwriter is more likely to get you the pricing you are looking for or even accept a submission rather than declining it if you the agent have information about the account and know what you're talking about. The moral of this story is to do your homework on your accounts before you initially contact them, during the application input process and when you go into the proposal.

Do your clients want the proposal delivered in person, by fax or on the internet? The answer to this question can tell you a lot about how serious the customer is about buying insurance from you. Meeting with the client face to face the first time is important. You can pick up a lot you miss from the phone and emails. I was at a proposal one time with a prospect and she had her

Farmers Workers' Comp policy sticking out of an envelope on her desk. When I had asked her initially whether she would like me get quotes on her work comp, she had said they were taken care of in that department. When I mentioned her work comp this time, she asked me, "Do you do workers' comp? My rates are out of control and I don't feel like anyone is watching my account." It turns out the agent had retired. If I had not gone out there to discuss my proposal I would have completely missed this company's work comp business.

Rounding out accounts is important to the client and to you. I don't need to tell you that, but the message bears repeating since agents including myself often don't ask about the client's other coverages. What does that mean to ask about other coverages?

Often you have to ask several times about other policies in order to get the opportunity to bid on them. You have to walk a fine line between being a good salesperson wanting to round out accounts and a greedy snake wanting to cut the other person out in order to get a few more bucks in your wallet. Walking that fine line comes down to reading your customer. However, you will get different signals from your customer at different times depending on the pricing of other policies, claims status and mood of the day. The best way to write the other lines of business is to be polite but persistent and keep asking how their other insurance is going.

One way not to make the sale is to trash the other agent. Sometimes the client in a longstanding relationship with their agent will be irritated by a situation but this can resolve itself usually with time. If you jump on the emotional bandwagon of the moment and proceed to bad mouth the agent to the client, when things blow over with that agent you will look bad. If the client brings up a problem they are having with their insurance program and you are being asked for advice, offer the client alternative solutions to the problem. That way you come off as a professional merely doing your job as opposed to slinging mud which never looks good. Sometimes the problem with the other agent involves a claim that is not going the way the client wants. It is either taking too long to settle or it has been denied unfairly in the client's eyes. This can be a major opportunity for you to write the business, but be careful, the shoe will be on the other foot and you will have claims issues with your client if you spend any amount of time in insurance.

CHAPTER 14: HANDLING CLAIMS

Your client calls you on a weekend saying the roof of his store caught fire. What do you do? Ignore the call and wait until Monday to call them back; call back immediately even though you don't know what to do; research the claim, where to turn it in, etc. and then call back the insured immediately? The answer surprisingly can be the first, to wait until you can contact the insurer on Monday morning when it is open and have accurate useful instructions for the insured. Once you have been in insurance for a while you will know what to do. If the client has been served with a summons and complaint on a Friday afternoon, your most important timeline is 30 days. The carrier has to respond in writing to the complaint within 30 days of your client being served or the plaintiff will receive a default judgment. This would be a major Errors and Omissions claim for you if you forgot about the claim and didn't turn it in to the insurer.

It is best to get complaints in to the company as soon as possible. But be sure to review the complaint before turning it in. Even if it is a claim you are sure that won't be indemnified or even defended by the company, turn it in anyway. If you don't you are setting yourself up for second guessing by a competing agent who reviews a client's loss history. At worst you will get sued by your client for not following their instructions. Remember you are their agent and you have to follow their instructions. But that doesn't mean you can't go on record in writing or in a conversation strongly urging your client to cease and desist in their course of action.

Getting back to the claim on a weekend or after hours, most carriers have a 24 hour claims reporting phone number. This doesn't mean anything will happen until it hits the desk of the examiner who usually works Monday through Friday. But you can help your client out who will remember you going the extra mile by calling back during your time off. You should call the client back immediately and tell them you are turning in the claim, but they probably won't get follow up until Monday. Some carriers have a place on their website to turn in claims.

Seems like a lot of work, doesn't it, handling claims in addition to producing business and running an agency? You bet. As an agency owner you have to be familiar with all areas of the business, especially those that directly affect your retention of business and reputation. Clients will remember claims in terms of how much you genuinely tried to help them and your professionalism which can include explaining the occasional claim declination. Not every claim is going to get paid. To tell your clients otherwise is just a snow job. Of course as sales people we have to maintain a good positive attitude with our clients but that doesn't mean lying to them. It feels good momentarily to give your clients news they want to hear, but ultimately they will be twice as mad at you for getting their hopes up and not delivering.

So getting into your clients claims rather than taking the easier way out of ignoring them is often thankless drudgery, however it pays off in the long run. Don't avoid claims because it is vague and others tell you it's not worth the trouble or the potential E&O; help your client! To be indispensable to your client you have to understand and work every aspect of your agency.

CHAPTER 15: DO EVERYTHING

I have made many sales because commercial clients tell me the following chain of events occur with their large agencies: A really good broker or broker team sells them the policy. They never hear from the crack broker and team again. A CSR is assigned to their account. The brokerage changes the CSR frequently. At the time of this writing emailing was replacing faxing. I have a little secret here. The insured doesn't mind if you email them proposals every year if you are keeping in touch with them throughout the year. For many clients constantly showing up burns them out. They have meeting after meeting and unless they are bored or you are the most exciting presenter in the world, the last thing they want is another one.

However this does not relieve you of your obligation to keep in touch with your client. My point is that the renewal should be another task you complete for them professionally and thoroughly. But it should not be the only time they hear from you or else you will get branded with the label of typical greedy salesman just in it for yourself. The only way you get your client's confidence that you are their go to guy for all matters regarding their insurance is to immerse yourself in their business and risk management aspects of their business. To get to this point you have to work hard on your client's account. So if you're doing this you don't have to sweat the renewal since it is a natural extension of your other efforts for your client. Win that renewal battle before it's even fought. It comes down to reading your client as to their preference for face to face meetings. And also knowing who you are and how you best work. If you are more of an internet communicator and you are prospecting someone who wants to see you every month for a lunch meeting, you should probably pass on this client. You know you're not going to change who you are for just one client and to pretend otherwise is disingenuous and greed driven, which will not lead to a long term mutually profitable relationship with your client.

One element of "doing everything" is taking care of the so called menial tasks which have to be done. Rose my wife used to file claims paperwork for the Workers' Compensation and all personal lines lines at the insurer where we worked. She would file so much, the files would take on a life of their own and run after her menacingly in her dreams. She would wear presentable office clothes even when she knew it would be a day of heavy filing. Her title was File Processor. She would of course grumble to herself about how badly this job sucked. When she picked in the fields as a kid, the grape paper where she deposited the grapes she picked would often slit her fingers and hands. Rose thought she was done with paper cuts after working in the fields. Not so. The paper files had come back to leave slits on her fingers yet again. Instead of complaining to management about how she hated her job, she would keep her thoughts to herself. Who would have known that she would be filing for our own insurance agency. She finally understood why she had to go through a job she hated because it taught her skills she would need in her own business. So don't avoid work because you feel you are better than those positions. Someday you may need these skills and instead of making money for someone else, you will be building your own future and your own business.

Another element of "doing everything" is having lunch or you and your family having dinner with your client. In other words you socialize with them as well as do business with them. Some clients keep a barrier between work and home life so you will never insinuate yourself into that part of their life nor should you try too hard. But most business people form relationships with their suppliers and their customers too so it is only natural that you should form some connection with your client. One of our cornerstone clients who is also my best friend has invited us to his kids' high school graduations. We have invited his wife and him to our birthday parties. We went to a concert together in Vegas. However, this happened over time. We are there for them if something comes up whether this is in life or strictly business.

If you are single you do not want to date your client because when your relationship hits the rocks so do your policies. If you are married it is nice to socialize with your client if they are a couple. Watch out for the sleazebags out there that will want to hit on your partner. You will want to hit them. You don't want these sleazebags for a client. My rule of thumb is would I want my client for a friend if I wasn't selling them something. If the answer if yes then I can socialize with them and not feel like a materialistic phony who is just out for a buck.

An old timer agent told me that he had one rule he applied to his customers. If he could see any of them in the grocery store and not duck into the cereal aisle to avoid them, he was doing his job. If he had to avoid anyone he was not meeting his own internal expectations. This is a good general rule with a qualification. You are going to have clients who are pissed off at you. It just goes with the territory. Maybe it has to do with a claim that didn't get paid. Maybe the claims adjuster peeked in the window at your client while they were taking a shower. Too many forms to fill out at audit. Client didn't know about a phone inspection. The potential aggravations are endless and you are on the hook for all of them. The cereal aisle test is more about integrity. Sure you are going to piss off some of your clients, but can you look them in the eye and know you have done your best for them? That's the test of success.

I am implying from the above that you don't have to be perfect to be successful, just indispensable to your client. A lot of the clients you work hard for and try to help will become your friends. If they don't become your friends they will probably at least keep their business with you. The main element is you and your effort. People can sense if you care about them and protecting their assets, capital and income with the insurance you buy for them. Care about your clients and they will care about you. But no matter how hard you work to be the go to for your client's insurance program, some will still leave you, and you will still go through periods of sales inactivity.

CHAPTER 16: GET THROUGH THE HARD TIMES WHEN YOU LOSE ACCOUNTS AND FAIL TO MAKE SALES

When I worked as a producer for a big commercial broker I would get monthly commission reports from the regional vp with "good job Scottie" jotted on it or "let's get moving" or nothing at all which was more ominous than an actual response. For some reason this would piss me off and terrify me at the same time that they were judging me monthly. The feedback irritated me because I was not impressed with how they produced or the supposed great resources they put at my disposal which was an illusion meant to get me to become an employee. I had succumbed to their sales pitch to work for them as a broker just like I was expected to get others to sign on with the company. One big sales job was how I came to see that company with very little service, expertise and resources to back up their bombastic claims. I resented their constant judging of me since I found them wanting in my judgment.

This how dare they judge me attitude has fueled a lot of people to start their own businesses. In my case I couldn't wait until I went out on my own. When you finally make the move the money you bring in becomes a very important number. But it is not tied any more to bragging rights or macho comparison games that you get in a brokerage. Sales managers play mind games and intentionally try to tie your commission to images of your self worth. They attempt to see what makes you tick and then link that number to whatever is important to you. And they are doing it because that is what they are told to do. And they are doing it to make themselves more money since the sales manager makes money on your back and on your book.

Well guess what, when you make the move to your own agency your commission no longer takes on any larger significance than the number you need to live. Isn't that ironic? When commission is how you survive it is not as important as executing for the client and retaining good relationships with your underwriters. This is because the manipulative head games your prior employer was attempting to play with you no longer matters as long as you never bought into it in the first place. And if you did completely buy into it you were probably also gullible enough to adopt wholeheartedly the "us v. them" mentality these companies try to foster to retain employees. If you felt this way you will probably not be reading this book.

Some agents adopt a strategy of going after a few large accounts if they have the training and a larger brokerage background. They reason that there is more revenue with these large accounts and less work involved rather than writing a number of smaller accounts. I disagree with this strategy for at least a couple of reasons. For one, there can be a lot of work involved with writing a large account and a lot of related costs. The related costs can be claims reviews and loss control which a large client expects. Unless you hire on a claims examiner and loss control engineer, you will have to subcontract out these services which you can pass on to the client. But sometimes in order to be competitive you cannot pass on these costs to the client. Another characteristic of these large accounts is that they get called on quite a bit by the competition. Slip up and there will be several other brokers ready to take your place. So you may need to pay for the extra loss control and claims review services out of the commission you make on the account which makes the large account less profitable.

Maybe the biggest reason I don't agree with the strategy of writing a few large accounts is the disproportionate significance these accounts will have to your business. If losing one could cause a serious economic damage to your agency I wouldn't risk it. Now it's a different story if you have a large number of smaller accounts and manage to land a whale. The whale is a great account to have as long as you don't ignore and lose your smaller accounts as a result. But if you only have a few large accounts, the severity of losing one is too great an exposure for your agency. Better to write a number of smaller and medium size accounts and spread out the types of accounts you are writing in order to disperse the concentration of accounts and avoid shutting down if you lose one or a group of accounts.

Most insurance buyers are savvy enough to realize how big of an account they are for you. A large account might drive you crazy because their service expectations of you and your agency. I passed on bidding on a large account because the CFO expressed the attitude that they wanted to be a very big fish to an agency and were not getting that with their current large regional broker. I wasn't interested in having to jump every time this guy called. If I could have stood that kind of subservient junk I would have stayed in the corporate world.

So you are faced with a seemingly mutually exclusive situation. Get close to your customers, care about them and work very hard for them. But don't get too close to them or it will cost you emotionally if they leave you for another agency. It happens all the time; customers leave for a lower price or because they are angry or disappointed with you for a whole host of potential reasons. Ask them why they are leaving if they give you the courtesy of a blow off call. See if you can save the account. If not, and usually by the time they have gotten the courage to call you, they are already out the door, move on and close the door on them for now. Wish them well and let them know you are there for them just as you have been all along for them as their agent. Then get off the phone. Don't tailspin. Go get another client. Go for a run or lift some weights or do a crossword or go to a bookstore. But don't wallow in your misery. It will pass. So get close enough to care and really care, don't fake it. But when they leave, grieve some but keep working and move on. Don't let them get the best of you by doing something destructive like getting wasted or yelling at them and looking like a crybaby. Your destructive acts will end up hurting you not the object of your anger. Faggedda about dem. Be tough and act like a cold eyed mobster and do what you need to for your business. In the long run you won't remember that client but you will remember your overreaction if act out foolishly after losing a client.

CHAPTER 17: WHEN YOU GET EMPLOYEES, REMEMBER HOW IT WAS WHEN YOU WERE ONE

The biggest difference I had after 3 years of being in business on my own was having my wife my come on as my accounting chief. Before that I wrote all the checks manually myself and kept my balance in the checkbook itself. My agency wasn't big enough to necessitate anything more. This is fine if you want to keep your agency at a certain revenue level. But most likely your revenues will grow the longer you are in business. As you grow you will need a Customer Service Representative for your accounts, maybe a receptionist and you might bring on other producers, claims specialists or a loss control rep. As your employee list grows make sure you complete the paperwork. Give them a W4 form, have them fill it out and return it to you. Consider having an employee handbook. In a small operation it doesn't need to be more than a few pages but it could get you out of hot water if there is ever an employment issue that results in litigation.

Try to put yourself in their shoes when you have issues that come up. It is so easy to start seeing employees as "them" and you as management with a wide gulf in between in terms of goals, attitudes, work ethic and behaviors. I have been at agency meetings and heard agency owners bemoan the crappy work ethic of their employees. True, you have to motivate your employees, but they have to know that you remember how it was to be one. It motivates employees to be consulted on decisions affecting the agency. Making employees stakeholders increases their involvement in the agency which makes people care more for what they are doing. Employees who have a piece of the action are motivated to put in the extra effort to be successful. This doesn't just mean money. If you are frank with your employees about the challenges your agency faces, they will appreciate your honesty and feel more a part of the family.

A good business has the feel of a working family, not a dysfunctional family everyone can't wait to be rid of after Thanksgiving dinner. You can tell if you have this environment by the 5pm test. If you can shoot a cannon through your office right at quitting time most days, you most likely have time servers or clock punchers. This is not necessarily because you have lazy unmotivated employees. It could be because of the environment you create with your management style. If you are secretive, arrogant and play favorites with your employees, your workplace will reflect the unpleasant atmosphere of intrigue and office politics. Just remember when you worked in someone else's agency. Did you enjoy being threatened to produce, having corporate monitor you, the obligatory meetings and annual picnics that had all the bonhomie of funerals? Do something different with your agency. Tell your employees what's happening in the business. Cut them in when times are good. And unfortunately cut them back when times are bad. Good people will ride out the profitable and slack times with you depending on the depth of your relationship with them and the necessity of the times. Don't beat yourself up if someone doesn't take the job you offer them or if they move to another agency just for the money. It happens all the time and remember the moves you had to make to start your own agency.

I have learned a lesson over the years regarding employees which is the same with clients. Employees come and go and you can't pin your life or future on them nor can you afford to be so emotionally connected to them that their departure will devastate you. In a word, don't take it personally if they turn you down for a job or leave your agency for another job. The same goes with clients. When I was younger it would drive me crazy trying to figure out why clients left me for another agent and company. What was so ineffective about my service or delivery that I didn't get this prospect or keep this customer. As time passes I learned that people make decisions based on factors you will never know. Don't try to figure each loss out, move on. If you are doing something wrong you will know because there will be a trend of clients leaving or prospects not going with you. If you are not getting prospects from a certain class of business maybe you don't have the right market. This should motivate you to find out the company that customers are going with and then to represent the company so you can make those sales. The same with existing accounts. You know if you screwed up that it might cost you a client. So what, move on. Lessons in failure sting and should cause you to never make the same mistake. Pain has a way of being the best teacher sometimes when it comes to retaining lessons. But if you are losing a number of clients chances are another company is writing the business cheaper. Most clients are gracious enough to tell you the name of the succeeding company and agent. Do your homework and get this company and get a copy of that policy. If you can't get the company have another carrier quote with the same coverages and try to get the pricing right.

CHAPTER 18: GETTING PERSONAL: THE POTENTIAL IMPACT OF BUSINESS ON YOUR LIFE AT HOME

My agency didn't almost cost me my marriage. I did. I expected to become partner and buy out the agency I was working for. Fortunately I was canny enough to negotiate a 2 year waiting period in my contract. However the experience at the end of 2 years when I forced the issue about agency ownership was so disorienting and disgraceful that it caused a profound change in me. I became suspicious of everyone. Including my wife. My extreme dissatisfaction with my situation in the agency carried over to my relationship with my wife. The upshot was I wanted to end the unpleasantness of the agency situation and I wanted mistakenly to end my marriage. One relationship was toxic, the other was my saving grace.

Some say that working too much can cost you your marriage. In my case, it helped and saved us. After my wife graduated with a degree from a local university, she came to work with me. We never looked back. When we work too much we are working together. We opened another location where my wife grew up and remodeled a building together with my sister and brother in law. We work, live and play together. Don't get me wrong, we have our own interests. I like to write and play golf while Rose hangs out with her sisters and friends and finds great ways to give back to the community. We have our own lives but we do most everything together because that turned out to be the solution to our problem. Rose fought for me and I fought for her and above all we allowed God to lead us in the direction of our life together. I did the wrong thing and it almost cost me marriage. No matter how fed up you become with your work situation, don't let it give you an excuse to do the wrong thing in your marriage.

CHAPTER 19: GIVE GIVE GIVE

When my wife was a little girl her dad had all 7 of her brothers and sisters picking in the fields during the summer. She lived in the barrio in a small wood frame house. No dishwasher of course, no dryer. The landlord would pick up the rent every week in person, a kindly old gentleman who did not look down on Rose's hardworking parents. My father in law was never late with the rent and never got a charge card, he didn't believe in debt. One of his many contradictions is that he found debt immoral but thought nothing of spending the money he made on the backs of his kids in the fields to buy rounds of drinks for everyone at the city pool hall.

The barrio is a collection of small houses with dogs chained up and kids running in the street. During the summer the swamp coolers make houses appear to be sweating in the 108 degree temperatures. What it really is is the water from the condensation dripping down the side of the house. Now you read about people who talk about escaping from their humble beginnings into some grand and important neighborhood, house and circle of friends. Not Rose. She always wanted to go back to her hometown and more importantly help the residents of the barrio. Every Christmas after we moved back, Rose gets someone to play Santa and dispense food and gifts to residents of the barrio where she grew up. She is not ashamed of her origins. She feels an obligation to give back to the community that gave to her the place of her childhood. It's a way of doing good right back after having it done to you to paraphrase the Auden poem in a slightly different way. When she was a kid Rose always remembered a man dressed up as Santa walking through the Barrio neighborhoods giving out a piece of hard candy and fruit to the kids who had lined the sidewalks to watch the scene and receive candy.

As minimal as a piece of candy and fruit seems today, Rose never forgot the gesture because it showed someone cared. Rose had nothing growing up in the way of toys so this was all she was getting for Christmas. When she got older she wanted to be the person who helped a little girl or boy feel the magic of a surprise, to feel loved and cared for by Santa. So the second year after we opened our office in Rose's hometown, we started giving out candy and fruit to the barrio residents before Christmas. Each year our Santa Barrio celebration has grown. The first year it was just Rose, her sisters and her sister's father in law playing Santa who participated. The second year people heard about the event and they magically appeared early to help pack the bags with fruit and candy. A generous produce broker donated the fruit and we bought the rest. Last year, we had a police escort, about 30 volunteers and newspaper coverage. The reason we have been able to do this is because of the business. It is a privilege and supreme benefit to be able to use the money we make to help others. It's easy to get wrapped up chasing the buck when it is so hard to earn a living, but don't forget to always give even if your profit margin is razor thin. It will pay off in terms of happiness and satisfaction. Looking at yourself in the mirror is easier when you sacrifice yourself for others.

CHAPTER 20: WHAT IS SUCCESS

Success can be measured in many ways. One sure fire way that many business people use is money. And why not? It is quantifiable yardstick of success. In insurance, sales are the lifeblood of our business. And measuring sales means measuring the premium dollar amounts of policies sold. But this section is not on how to measure success but more on what success has meant to me and more importantly what success costs.

I think the most obvious by product of success whatever that means is happiness or satisfaction. When I opened my own agency in December 2001 and I put my desk, chair and bookcase together, it was with satisfaction that I sat behind my desk for the first few times. I thought to myself, "Wow, this is owning an agency, how sweet is this." As I mentioned in an earlier chapter I was going about life the wrong way, and I don't think I would have been able to keep the agency open had I continued what I was doing. I was divided, working devilishly hard on my business but not investing in my homelife, looking for what I thought I wasn't getting there in other places.

No doubt about it, I had to make some changes or my newfound agency that I felt such satisfaction about was headed toward a cliff and into the abyss.

The essence of what happened is I began to sacrifice to make the agency work. I got my life with my wife and business together, committing to both fully after wavering. This harmony of purpose helped me to have the character to withstand the problems that inevitably come with starting a new agency. One of those problems were tactics by the previous agency where I worked. For instance the agent sent a letter to a longstanding client of mine telling them how much I "charged" them in commission and that he would write their business for significantly less money. The client handed me this letter with a sad shake of her head. Nothing needed to be said. Dirty pool tactics made him look bad, not me. Always remember that if you get in a conflict with another agent it makes you look just bad if you descend to their level. The best revenge is to open up your agency and make a success of it. I left that sad environment that morning and never looked back. The agency owner tried to physically restrain me from taking my items from my desk. I may be 5'7" but in college I was a boxer and took my self restraint not to put him on the floor. I did not sue, I did not call the police: I had a business to start.

This was the beginning of December and a very miserable cold time, the perfect reflection of what I felt inside. Word traveled quickly that I was out on my own and several agency owners called me to see if I would be interested in coming aboard. One interview I had occurred in a restaurant in Castroville. It was pouring outside and this partner of a big chain of agencies told me I should come work there. He would put a desk in his office for me. He wanted to know the minimum I could exist on which would be my draw until my commissions began. Gee thanks but no thanks I politely told him. I told him this was my opportunity to start my own agency and if I didn't do it now I would probably never do it. To his credit after he saw his pitch didn't work and noted my resolve, he agreed with me and said he would do the same in my situation. While I was talking with him my resolve did grow and I knew what I was going to do. Always talk through your decisions before you make them. It helps to crystallize your thoughts and suddenly everything can become very clear as it did for me in this situation.

So I had an external enemy, but I also had an enemy in the mirror by not doing things the right way in my life and not having harmony in my family and business life.

The concrete steps to success that I followed were:

1) Saying the rosary every day with my wife

2) Continuing not to drink

3) Getting up early on Sunday and going to church instead of sleeping in

4) Giving up coffee

5) Giving up nicotine

My brother was working on starting his own business and we were discussing the formative stage activities. He said yeah it was easy for you though, you just did it and your business took off. Well not exactly bro. I told him that whatever little success I have had has been due to the sacrifices I have made. Without sacrifice I am certain I would have failed in my business. Without going to church and believing in God my marriage would have failed. I have no agenda for your conversion here other than emphatically stating that you have to give things up to succeed, that success comes with a price and that price is sacrifice.

CHAPTER 21: GO IT ALONE

The essence of owning your own business is the willingness to do the opposite of what others are telling you to do sometimes. It's harder than it sounds to go against conventional wisdom. Remember that less than 10% of the population has ever started their own business. Going with the grain is working for someone else in a larger company that presents the illusion of security. Conventional wisdom is taking no risks and keeping your goals low and being satisfied with not trying anything new. For all this generation's lip service about individuality and seizing the day, it is mostly a fashion reference or a marketing slogan to get you to buy something.

At one point I had everyone and I mean everyone telling me to join up in a large agency and work as a partner there. The pay was good, the people were top of the line and the security was tangible. However, I would have had to answer to 6 other partners if I wanted to pursue a new line of business, get an appointment with a new carrier, or make any major changes at the agency. If something goes wrong with a claim, I have 6 people to answer to. If I land a whale, I have to cut in 6 other people. This did not appeal to me as it probably does not appeal to you if you have read this far.

The owner of a large regional agency group walked into my office when I started and told me if I didn't sell my agency to him he would put me out of business, that an individual agent cannot make it. I asked him when he started if he considered working for someone else. He told me it was different now. I asked him how? A good independent agent can make it on his or her own. That's what he did. What a hypocrite telling me to sell out to him when he never sold out to anyone. The agency still had his name on the door. I gave him my best go straight to hell smile and he stopped calling soon after.

One of the best moments as an independent agent is when you feel the thrill of the chase after doing the hard work of getting the lead, surveying the risk, identifying and analyzing the loss exposures and apping out the risk for the markets. You have done your work and now it's time to discuss with the underwriters the pricing you will need to land the account. You get your quotes, present them to the insured and if you have a shot, you wait expectantly for the good word. It gets interesting when the other agent comes in with their numbers. Sometimes they don't even know you're quoting. If you have done your work well, you will surprise them with your quote and recommendations.

Many times the reaction of the competition is very predictable and follows a pattern. First they will tell your future client they have never heard of you in order to marginalize you. Then they will tout the virtues of how big they are, the size of their office, the number of employees. This is complete bullshit since an agent typically writes an account and then passes it off to their CSR. That makes 2 people at most who really know the account. And judging from the incompetence and lack of knowledge of a lot of the agents out there, usually that makes one with knowledge of the account. Finally if their smokescreen and slanderous comments fail they will ask for last shot and if they can go back to the underwriter for pricing.

As an independent, see yourself as a guerilla with face paint on, waiting at the edge of the forest to beat the other agent. They will not hesitate to take your accounts, so make sure you return the favor to the biggest jackals among them. Prepare for resistance. I was competing for an account once and the incumbent agent told the client I did not have an office, that the address on my business card was bogus. Needless to say my next appointment with my new client was in my office instead of his. This proved I followed through on what my business card said. It also made the other agent look desperate, incompetent and weak. I got the business.

Prepare for your competitors' criticism of you as a lone wolf with nobody in your office and no office support. Make this your greatest strength. Your client will always know it is you working on their account and you take 100% responsibility for it; there is no passing the buck. But clients like accountability and being able to get through to someone time after time after time. Predictability in the way of good service means repeat business. Try to keep your same address and contact information. You are fighting an uphill battle that you can win against the other agents who say you have no resources and are not big enough to take care of your client's insurance needs. Refute this argument by what you say and more importantly what you show time after time, month after month, year after year. Be stable; don't change your phone number all the time or your office. Your clients appreciate stability and predictability with you. You are an extension of the policies you sell. Just as the policies you sell reduce uncertainty for your clients so the way you conduct yourself should instill confidence in your clients and not give them reason to worry.

CHAPTER 22: WHAT THE COMPETITION IS SAYING ABOUT YOU

To beat you the competition is telling your customers and prospects lots of belittling half truths about you. The first thing they say is that you are too small to be effective. This is the standard dig and I wish those agencies would show more imagination. This is probably the easiest criticism to counter. Fact is, after the agent sells the account there is one person who will be servicing the client's account, the customer service representative. In other words there will be one person maybe two working on the client's account whether at your agency or at a large mega broker. And you can turn this criticism right back on the other agency. You can say that a licensed successful agent and not a CSR will be working on the account. Sell your expertise always. After all you are on your own because you are good enough to go it alone. Don't let the competition use your strength against you!

Take your competitor's criticism and turn it right back on them. They say you are too small to effectively represent the client to the markets. You tell your client that they are too large to care. Tell your client they are a big fish in your agency and will receive special attention. To the other agency they will be just another client and probably not all that important to their business plan. Tell them that the broker who looks so good selling the policies is most likely instructed to move on after the account is sold. You do not employ a "hit and run" philosophy like your competitor. The work for you begins once the sale is made. Too many times the large producer writes an account and passes it off to their CSR to service while the producer goes for another sale barely remembering the customer if they see them around town. Tell your customer or prospect that you will work their account all year long, monitor it for changes, talk to them when they need something and stay up to date on coverages and how they relate to your customer's insurance program. I was playing golf with a client and he was talking about a job they recently completed. He couldn't remember the job name which I filled in for him. He looked startled and asked, "How did you know that?" I replied it was because I did the cert for the general contractor and job owner. When you show your client that you are invested in their business by staying on top of their account, they are much less likely to listen to big brokers and the derogatory comments they make about you in order to get the business.

CHAPTER 23: MAKE FRIENDS NOT ENEMIES

One of the reasons I was able to start my agency and keep it going was the goodwill of others. With the exception of maybe one agent and one agency, I have remained on good terms with people in the insurance business. You have to earn this goodwill and you do it by helping out your colleagues when you can and that means even when it costs you money or a client. You can compete hard with an agent for a piece of business but once it's over, let it go. Case in point when I left an agency for another position in the 90's there were some hard feelings and tough times as that agency competed with me to retain my business. They kept some of it, though I retained the great majority of it based on the strength of my client relationships. But after I went out on my own this company actually gave me a number of accounts, files and all. We took care of it quietly and I was grateful to the guy in charge for transferring the book to me. He didn't have to help me, but he did and I am grateful for his generosity. With time we stopped competing for business so often, and I held no hard feelings toward my previous employer. This would not have been the case just a couple of years previously.

Some agents will exasperate you with their seeming desperation to steal your business. But consider how you get many of your accounts. Not all of them were new ventures. We are all trying to make money to put food on the table for our families. And it takes a competitive spirit to make it. But that does not mean you have to hate your competitors. At the end of the day even after that business is written or lost, the other agency will still be there. And someday you may want to place business through them or hire the producer who competed with you or worst case go to work for them if your agency does not work out. If you burn your bridges with other agencies you eliminate the possibility of future mutually beneficial dealings. If the agency is stealing client money or taking advantage of their clients you do not want to associate with them. But that does not mean you trash them to prospects or clients. Keep it factual and move on to positive issues about what you can do for your client not how they are being screwed by their current agent. That is bad business and it will catch up with you.

So you have made a great friend in the insurance business, referred a lot of business back and forth and seem to be the ideal fit from a personality and business standpoint. Both of you decide while you are working at the same agency or at different agencies that you want to start your own shops. How about if you pool expenses and revenues and start up as a partnership? I would say to be very very cautious about partnerships especially during the fledgling stage of your agency. Listen, you will have plenty of time to partner up at any time you wish down the line after you establish yourself. But the reverse is not equally true. It could be hard to extricate yourself from a bad partnership and that could cost you lots of time, aggravation, clients and revenue. Don't succumb readily to the temptation to have a buddy there during the uncertain time of starting your business. It seems like it could help to ensure your success when it might be ensuring nothing but trouble in the future. If you want to run with someone else, maybe you should keep your revenues separate but hold yourself out as a partnership. This is the truth if your partnership consists of two colleagues who work in the same space and write different types of coverage for the same clientele. For instance you write the P&C and your partner writes health insurance. This combination sets up the possibility of you each prospecting the other's book of business for different lines of business. It insulates your client from the competition if you and your partner write all of your client's insurance. The convenience factor for your client can't be underestimated when it comes to insurance. Many clients want to be able to call one phone number for their insurance needs. This is a powerful selling point with existing clients as well as prospects. But.....there are some potential drawbacks with this approach.

For one thing, there is no natural link between health insurance and property-casualty. The two types of coverage are separate in the minds of insureds. I have found time and time again that clients choose different agency representation for their health and property-casualty lines. That doesn't mean that the same agent or agency cannot write both types of coverage it just means that writing one line doesn't automatically lead to the next. The significance of this is that if you are considering bringing in a partner to write life and health, don't make the mistake of assuming that you will pick up the P&C on this book. I had a colleague who envisioned cocooning his life and health accounts by cross selling Property and Casualty coverages through referrals to a P&C agent. Did it work? There were some hits, certainly, but not enough to justify a partnership. A partnership to share office expenses is a good reason for a P&C and life and health agent to open up a shared office. But they should not count on mining each other's book of business as a solution to saving a sagging book of business. If you pool revenue and expenses make sure your commission volumes of business are about the same or differentiate between the commission from your book and theirs to avoid problems later if one's book grows or diminishes out of proportion with the other.

CHAPTER 24: AVOIDING E&O'S AND LAWSUITS

You would think that as insurance agents we would be the best protected from lawsuits and losses. But because agents are always designing risk management programs for clients many times we let our ultimate client down, ourselves, with often disastrous results. Like the overweight doctor who smokes, we preach well to our clients but often we are not the practicers of our risk management faith. So let's discuss some easy steps to minimize your errors and omissions exposure since this is one of the greatest risks we face in our business. Then we can talk about about other hazards and how to control them if we can't eliminate them.

The most common errors and omissions claim comes from forgetting to add a piece of property or a vehicle to an insured's policy. Who hasn't been busy, taken a call on a Friday afternoon when you have one foot out the door and completely forgotten about the conversation once you've hung up...well you should be saying, "I haven't forgotten!!!" If you have though, do one thing, keep a piece of paper next to your desk and write the note down even if you know you won't forget to add it. And then add it again on your agency management system or in Outlook as another reminder in case that paper burns up while you are at home or flies away. Most management systems have note functions on each client that is handy for that double check method I just discussed. You can type into the record a reminder to make that change and pend it for 30 days. An easy way to follow up on receipt of endorsements is to keep a pending folder on your desk. It only works if you actually check it though. Failure to add property and vehicles are the easiest E&O's to avoid and the easiest mistakes to commit. A good paper and computer system should eliminate those issues.

Another type of E&O that can lead to trouble is more subtle. This has to do with coverage a client doesn't have at the time of a claim. For instance, you write an office and do not notice that the carrier has put a designated premises endorsement on the policy. This eliminates coverage for claims that originate away from the premises. As a practical matter it means your client doesn't have products and completed operations coverage. You can solve this by reading through those policies you get. Is there any greater charge than getting a policy with your name as agent on it? No, I didn't think so, or you wouldn't be reading this book. But go one step further when you are admiring that policy with your agency name on it and review it for gotcha endorsements such as this. Chances are the busy underwriter will not let you know it is on there when they quote. And most companies put disclaimers on their quotes now that say the quote may differ from coverages and limits requested.

Another subtle type of errors and omissions claim can occur with claims that arise from the past. Watch those claims made forms. Note that your present carrier's coverages on a claims made policy is the coverage for all policy periods from the retroactive date to the present. So if you have more restrictive coverage on your present policy than the last company and a claim pops up from a preceding policy period your client will have less coverage for that new claim. As an example, say you have a contractor on a claims made form. The first policy you write has no exclusion for work on tract homes. The second policy you write has an exclusion for tract homes. Your client makes a product which goes into a tract home but they do not install it.

The problem occurs if there is a construction defect claim on that work which was completed during the period of the policy with broader coverage. It doesn't matter when the work was completed. The policy which will respond is the current one due to the claims made nature of coverage. Since it contains an exclusion for tract work, your client is out of luck and you may face an E&O claim even though you had the correct coverage when the work was done. Unlike an occurrence policy claims made policies no longer respond to any claims at the end of the policy period unless you renew them or buy the tail or supplemental extended reporting period. This is not to say to avoid claims made policies at all costs. Sometimes you cannot avoid them. Directors' & Officers' Liability, Employment

Practices Liability are almost always written on a claims made basis as are a lot of general liability policies with long timeline products exposures such as construction or medical products. Note that the policy in force will govern claims for all policy periods covered under this policy even if the occurrence took place before the inception date of the policy.

Another issue with claims made occurs when the insured cancels or moves coverage to an occurrence form. You must offer your client an extended reporting period policy. The current insurer will offer the basic extended reporting form period to the insured at no additional cost. This affords 60 days after the policy expires in which to report occurrences from the previous policy period. For a premium equal to 1 year of premium usually you should offer your client the extended reporting form which in effect allows the client to make claims on occurrences from the claims made policy period up to 5 years or with some, indefinitely. Get your client to acknowledge their refusal of an extended reporting form option preferably in writing. If not at the very least send them a letter that they have refused the offer from the carrier to extend their reporting period. Keep the letter in their file and have a nice life. Don't do it and risk seeing their lawyer in court. Some other situations that you want to confirm in writing with your client is a deletion of an auto, property or changing of limits. It seems so basic but note all changes in the insured's file, whether you tfile electronically or still use paper files, make sure you document. At one of the brokerages where I worked there was a separate Errors and Omissions specialist whose job it was to investigate and handle potential coverage problems with insureds. He told me that the difference between a good agent and a great agent is documentation. Keep a record of all changes with your client's policies. Send them letters, faxes and emails acknowledging the change or better yet the endorsement itself. Ask if they have questions just in case they don't remember making the change. If a couple is getting a divorce you will get calls occasionally to take a vehicle off because the spouse doesn't want to pay for the estranged one's insurance any longer. Be careful with this because the car is still in both of their names until the decree is issued and the divorce becomes final. Communicate with both parties before you follow the advice of one and acknowledge in writing what you have done.

CHAPTER 25: COMMISSIONS & CONTINGENCIES

The lifeblood of agencies is its customers. And with customers come commission revenue. If you worked for another agency as an agent without a piece of the action you were probably never told about contingent income. This type of revenue is a hallmark of the independent agency system. The way it works is at the end of the year the insurer tallies up your premium written and loss ratio for the year. Usually there is a minimum premium threshold you have to hit in order to qualify for contingencies. This number varies from company to company. For lines of business that are more specialty and typically represent less premium volume such as mobile homes/motorcycles/ATV insurance, the threshold is much lower and can be as low as $50,000 in premium. You can instantly tell what mode a carrier is in by their contingency plan. Some are ridiculously complicated with calculations based on new and renewal business with premium growth factored in to the final number. The companies that want to grow and write new business will reward new business and de emphasize loss ratio. There is a correlation between new business and losses. The more you grow in premium usually the more losses you will have in your book. A company that is treading water and not looking to grow will reward low loss ratio and will not incentivize new business growth if it increases loss ratio. If you have large losses you will most likely not qualify for contingency commissions whether or not the company is in growth mode. Continue that pattern and carriers will send out their marketing reps to have solemn talks with you about pulling up your numbers. In other words, you will have your appointment terminated if you don't turn things around.

Companies do their contingency calculations on a calendar year basis. Losses are incurred or paid plus reserved. Most P&C companies do not trend losses or include a loss development factor since reserves are theoretically where losses will end up. Incurred but not reported claims are not factored in either. These are factors that are elements of Workers' Compensation loss reserving practices. Workers' Comp carriers do not pay contingencies with few exceptions. If you are writing retrospective rating plans on incurred or paid bases, then IBNR and LDF's become critical to determining how much your client will receive after the first calculation by the carrier. Sometime in the fourth quarter around October the company will send you an offer for insurance. In return for lower contingencies you can lock in your loss ratio guaranteeing your contingency number no matter what happens with your clients' losses for the rest of the year. If you know or have a gut feeling that losses will occur in the last 3 months of the year it is a good call to take the carrier's offer of insurance. If not you can make substantially more, usually around 15%, by going without the carrier's guarantee. As I mentioned losses are calculated as paid plus reserved. The incurred loss numbers often grow at the end of the year. Underwriting departments do reviews of their book of claims at the end of the calendar year. It is no coincidence that reserves are reviewed and often increased at the same time that contingencies are calculated since higher reserves directly affect the payout by the companies. Check your loss runs with each company at the end of the year. Stay up on those open claims. Not doing it will cost you money. You may not win every battle with claims but you will get some reserves lowered and catch some glaring errors that you wouldn't have seen if you didn't take a look at those loss runs.

So if you have a reasonably good year in terms of new business and your loss ratio is under 40% or 60% depending on the line of business, you should make about 3% additional commission. So if you made 15% commission, with contingencies your commission will be 18% because you have received an additional 3 % in contingent income. Occasionally you will hook up with a carrier that wants to write more business and will incentivize new business growth. You can make more with those companies. A caveat is not to move your best accounts to these companies just to make a buck. After you move all your business to this company and receive the first year growth bonus, you will be penalized for renewal business the next year because your growth will be way off. Live by the incentive and die by the incentive. Forget what the companies are telling you about growth being more important than steady rational growth. This is benefitting the vice president of marketing, not your clients. The company contingency plans will change, but your customers will not. They will not appreciate being moved around from company to company to fatten your wallet or because you want to please the company. Sometimes the marketing rep does such a good job selling the company line of new business production uberalles that you buy in and move your clients to those companies. You will probably only do this once because the next year chances are the marketing rep will be emphasizing stability, read: the company grew too fast and losses outpaced profit, and all that business you troubled yourself and your clients to move will be stuck there in a company that is no longer rewarding production. Bottom line is only move your client's business to companies if first it is best for the client. Contingencies can be tempting but do not move business just to amass more premium volume if it is not in the best interests of your client.

CHAPTER 26: PROSPECTING AND SURVEYING

One of the hardest things about insurance production is how to find your customers. Many insurance people are so aggressive about asking people for their business that prospecting at a funeral home for life insurance policyholders would not seem unreasonable to them. And if you are an agent and these over the top hucksters know that, they will lobby you to work for them. Behind their eyes you see one color, green. They have your money on their mind and their mind on your money.　Nothing quite so repels me as a salesperson who is inappropriately aggressive. They are the flip side of the customer who has loss after loss and then blames the agent for not getting a better renewal deal. Both are repellent, and I often wonder if that's the kind of customer such aggressive tactics yield. If people know you are desperate you will get customers who take advantage of you.　So where is the best place to prospect? I am not contradicting myself really by saying wherever you happen to be. You can prospect without being craven in the grocery store, at your kids' football games, your non profit organization you volunteer for, and yes even at church, if it is done at the appropriate time. Letting people know what you do is not that hard as long as you don't become obnoxious about it like dropping your business card at every opportunity.

Once people know what you do and that you have solved the insurance problems of many many of your customers, they will come to you later on when they have a problem. Or if you stress how much money you save your average client, if they get a renewal that seems high, you will have planted a suggestion that will come to them when they are ready to shop their coverages. The best sale is no sale at all. You solve the problem or meet the need of the customer and the sale becomes inevitable, just another part of the service process you initiated after your customer came to you for help. The best way to get prospects is through referrals from existing clients. One referral is worth ten cold calls. Usually in business insurance referrals go from one person in the industry to another. For example, if a landscaper is unhappy with their insurance program, they will most likely call another landscaper to see who they are using. So if you get a few insureds in the same business ask them for referrals.

Another referral source is trade associations. Join an association of businesses whose insurance you have written or would like to write. Get active in the association and advertise in the directory. Ask the folks in the office to refer you to people who call the association looking for insurance. Most likely you will find yourself joining an association with several other insurance practitioners. Go to an annual meeting and see if the agents have a trade show booth there. If not, get a booth the next year and ask the association to give a talk to members about an insurance topic or coverage. With employment issues in the forefront of the news and popular media, you could discuss labor issues. At the same time that you discuss the exposures, you could discuss the treatment of them through insurance such as Employment Practices Liability Insurance. Use social networking sites if you are comfortable with them to advertise your agency. For instance you can advertise your agency's expertise in homeowners insurance on a social networking site if the demographic is young and newly married. I would watch the return on those advertising dollars very closely and make sure you keep a record of how many customers came to you because of this ad.

CHAPTER 27: FIND THE RIGHT VENDORS TO PARTNER WITH

You should choose your vendors, accountant, advertising, lawyer with the same care and diligence your clients exercise when they go through the process of selecting their insurance agent. Some agency owners pick accounting firms with exorbitant rates because their services are too important to the future of the agency to entrust to someone of uncertain pedigree. The same could be said about you the agent. If your clients when you started hadn't taken a chance on you, an unknown entity at the time, how would you have gotten your start? They say the higher rates must indicate greater expertise. The drawback to selecting the higher priced firms is that you might be a small fish to them and get the junior level practitioner on your account. Or their high hourly rates result from the cache of their name or how long the firm has been around.

A better way to select your vendors is to find someone to partner with over the life of your business. Finding someone just like you when you began in business with the ambition to rise by taking excellent care of their clients is not easy but it just takes time. Find someone who does things the way you do. First of all talk to other agents and find out who they are using. Ask your clients as well. When calling the referrals get some basic information from them and meet with them to see if it's a fit. Chances are a lawyer won't meet with you without charging so invite them to lunch and pick up the tab while you get to know them. These are long term relationships so don't be swayed by an attractive hourly rate at first to lure you into the firm. I know of one accounting company that gets you in with a guaranteed low hourly rate for the first year. By the next year your account gets transferred to a junior accountant and the rates increase. They figure after a year you are less likely to move your business because of the hassle involved in changing CPA's.

It is an even bigger hassle to choose the wrong partners. But if you have made a mistake or the situation has changed with your accountant, lawyer, business card printer, etc. such as them not returning your calls in a timely way or changing their schedule to three days a week, don't be afraid to start the process of finding someone else. Don't pay for the name of the firm. Find someone who understands insurance and agency operations. They should come out to your office and see your operations. If they can't be bothered to do at least that initially, what kind of service are you going to get down the line when you need their time or if something unexpected comes up and you need service immediately. Here's a test. Call the person handling your advertising or accounting on a Friday afternoon about 4:30 and see how long it takes to get a call back. Standard is Monday morning. If you get a call back that day or God forbid they are actually in the office or answering their cell, then you have some who will be attentive to your agency's needs.

Make sure you get along with the person or people you are partnering with. If you have an aversion to them from the start, chances are over time you will not like them any better. Avoid people who try to hard sell you or intimidate you into going with them. Such blowhards are not worth your time no matter how attractive their pricing or competent their work. Trust your gut if you are getting a bad feeling during the initial interview despite the good reviews you have received from your colleagues.

Pricing is an important component of any vendor relationship. Getting along very well with your accountant or printer or computer specialist can make it awkward to negotiate pricing. Maybe you went to high school or college with them. Get their hourly rate. Also get another quote even if you are dead set on a particular company or person. Your clients make you compete for their business, your vendors should compete for yours too. Competition enables you to get the best deal by allowing you to compare and contrast the pricing, services and background of the various people and firms you interview. Also, each vendor brings something different to the table in the way of knowledge, skills and experience. They can give you helpful ideas about running your business.

So get multiple looks at each service you outsource. Accounting is very important because of the fiduciary nature of our duty as holders of customer funds. Trust accounts cannot be touched and if you have no control of your banking, you could lose your license and get sued by your companies and clients. The same goes for your computers. Unless you are very experienced in computers, information systems, network servers you should outsource your computer services to a third party vendor. Hourly rates vary widely in this type of business so get a range of quotes and references. You are effectively stuck when your internet goes down. You need someone who will respond quickly and effectively when you have a problem such as a virus or an internet interruption. If you use the "cloud" computing concept of Applied TAM online, you have another resource of live online chat help features as well as a toll free helpline to call. Who to use for phone service is an important call you have to make. Get a toll free 800 or 888 number for your clients to call so they don't have to spend money to contact you over the phone. It's the small things like this that shows consideration for your clients. It won't get you the business but not doing it will reflect negatively on you.

Agency websites are a must. But this doesn't mean you must spend a fortune on them. You can partner with a graphic artist who specializes in website design and customization. Be prepared to supply most of the content yourself and to spend several hours on the phone and meeting with your designer. And once your website is complete you still must pay a maintenance fee to have your agency listed on search engines. If you want to do it yourself there are several applications out there to help such as Yahoo's Site Builder. Make sure you know what you are doing before you publish your website. A pathetic user-unfriendly website gives the impression to visitors that your agency is run the same way. Unless you are selling insurance and linking up with your companies through hyper text buttons, you don't have to present the world's most elaborate website to the public. One that functions, looks good and leads customers to contact you is a good website in my opinion. Be prepared to spend at least $1,000 on your website and you can spend much much more.

Should you try to write the insurance business of your vendors? You bet. But there are issues to consider. If you are providing the insurance to your vendor you might be less inclined to negotiate hard when it comes to rates. This is not a big deal because most professionals have a set rate schedule which they charge all their clients. You get the rates they charge to others. The problem can occur when you want to change vendors. You might be hesitant to switch because you don't want to lose the insurance business you write for them. Instead of switching consider correcting the problem before you make a move. That way, if the rates do increase unfairly or the service does not improve you know you gave your vendor the opportunity to correct the problem before you yanked the business.

CHAPTER 28: HAVE A SUCCESSION PLAN FOR YOUR BUSINESS

When you are in your 20's and 30's the last thing you are thinking about is retirement. Hell, you're just trying to make it in your business. The endgame is not even a consideration when you are fighting so hard for survival and to make a go of it. Hit 40 though and you start getting whispers of a future when you won't want to work so hard and beyond that of a time when you won't be working at all. Sound risk management which you recommend to your client applies to you in this situation as well. Start saving in your 20's and 30's for your retirement. When you are building your book the amount you put aside with each paycheck will be small, especially when you first open your agency. When you work for an agency you probably will have participated in an employer sponsored 401 (K) plan. But there is no employer but yourself to look to when you start your own agency. And in the face of the difficulties and turbulence of starting and getting your business going, it is very easy to mentally omit or put off planning for your retirement.

There are more immediate reasons as well to put aside money. You could become incapacitated by an accident or disease. What would you do for income for your family then? Take some time to think through the possible scenarios of you having an accident or getting sick and not being able to work your agency. If you are just starting out you might not have employees to carry on the day to day operations of the agency. Or if you do have a CSR and producers, how would they feel continuing the agency without you at the helm. Would some jump ship? Would you feel comfortable handing over the operations of your agency to someone else while you recuperate? You need to think clearly about whether your clients would stay on. Since your service is the hallmark of your business, how could you blame your clients for not leaving if you are not able to maintain the level of attention you have been providing?

Most of the attention in perpetuation focuses on what happens in the event of the retirement of the principal. This can be methodically planned and saved for through a retirement account such as a SEP or IRA. But you dying or getting too sick to work presents a whole host of difficulties that you need to think about and plan for.

In the event of your death there should be a life insurance policy to enable your spouse to continue their way of life. This means the limit should be enough to pay off your house and those expenses which would be unmanageable for your spouse. If you get sick and can't work the ideal coverage to have is disability insurance. Buy as much of this type of insurance as you can. However it is very expensive since it replaces lost income. When you're starting out it might not be feasible to purchase. In that case you will want to have a buy sell agreement with another agency. The trigger event for this agreement should be your death or incapacity.

How effective this agreement is depends on whether the other party will honor it and their ability to do so. It helps to have a legal contract spelling out the terms of the agreement. Be sure you are picking an agency which mirrors your service commitment and way of doing business. Many agreements pay something like 125% the first year of renewal commissions, 75% the second year and 50% of the third year commissions. Note that your spouse only gets paid if your clients renew with the successor agency so it is in your interest to make sure that it is a fit for your clients in the new agency. It is also a good idea to prepare clients by casually dropping the other agency's name in a complimentary way. You should have a formal or informal non compete agreement with that agency so that you don't become competitors after you disclose your book of business to the other agency.

You could even arrange the buyout to be funded by Key Man life insurance if the other agency is uncertain about how much business will come over to them following your death. The other agency buys the policy and pays the premium and so they are the owner of the policy and you are the life insured. You should not go too high on the limit. It is never a good idea to give businesspeople you don't know that well a financial incentive to whack you! But seriously, if they want a very high limit, beyond their expense level in assigning an agent and CSR to your book, then you should look for another agency with which to make your buy sell agreement. Otherwise you might as well just have your spouse taken care of by life insurance proceeds from a policy you purchase on yourself. Be fair to your clients though and have a succession plan for the business even if you are not concerned about the revenue from the transferred accounts. Key man life insurance works very well when you have a buy sell agreement with another agent or agency. My above example only considered you agreeing to transfer your book after your death or incapacity to another agency without them reciprocating in the event of their dissolution.

If it is a two way deal between you and another agent or agency you can very effectively fund that purchase of the book with life insurance proceeds. Find a life insurance business partner you refer business to and who refers business to you and have them place two key man life policies for you. Draft an agreement with legal counsel that clearly spells out who gets what under what circumstances so that there is no confusion once the event occurs triggering the agreement. You don't want your spouse to have to go to court to recover or simply get screwed out of the funds you worked so hard to provide for your family. The last thing a grieving spouse should have to do is to chase down what's owed to them especially since you have probably promised that they will be taken care of.

When I went out on my own, my planning for this contingency was one of the first things I told my wife in order to alleviate her concerns should something happen to me. Think this through before you open your agency and it will save you a lot of time and heartache later. Even if you don't have the perfect other party to transfer your book to at first, at least have a plan and fill in that person or agency later.

CHAPTER 29: FINDING THE RIGHT MIX OF BUSINESS

What is the correct proportion of Commercial Lines and Personal Lines and Employee Benefits in an agency? There is no absolute answer to this question. If you started as primarily a commercial lines agent then most likely the majority of your agency's book will be commercial lines. However you may branch out to other lines of business by design, by chance or due to client requests. If your book is shrinking in whatever line you write or specialize in, you may decide to expand your writings to another line of business such as personal lines or health insurance. A good way to go about this is to do your research ahead of time rather than just start writing policies without any idea of target customers. If for instance you decide to write personal lines insurance and begin to write some of your commercial clients' home and auto, you stand a chance of losing all of their business if you are clueless about what you are writing.

Take an insurance course online or attend a personal lines seminar of which there are many and which will come with the side benefit of state continuing education credits. Go on Insurance Brokers Association or American Institute of Chartered Property Casualty Underwriter's websites if study at home is what you are looking for or look for classes in the field you want to enter. Also, call some agents you are not competing with to get their take on that end of the business. There is nothing like talking to someone who has actually made sales, experienced losses and is servicing a book of the type of business you want to write. They can save you some time in terms of hot companies to get appointed with, coverages to steer clear of and how to make your pitch and approach yield the maximum number of sales. Then jump in and start making calls, prospecting and writing business. Give yourself enough time to make a comprehensive assessment of whether this is a type of insurance you will continue to pursue and make a part of your marketing efforts. Don't forget to notify your E&O insurer if it's a line you didn't tell them you were going to write.

Another way you might start writing another line of business is by chance. A call from someone out of the blue could come in and you happen to take it at the right time. It might turn out to be a type of business you have never written before, whether it is the type of risk or the type of coverage they want. Early on in my career I wrote a roller coaster manufacturer and several of their suppliers. I found this insured by cold calling them. I had no idea what they did. I had gone to the library and looked up manufacturers in my area on D&B Microcosm. They appeared as a small manufacturer. Nothing could have prepared me for that ride, but it was well worth it and I met wonderful people in the business. You never know how you are going to embark on a new direction in your business. You can initiate it or it can happen by chance. Either way can be equally effective and fulfilling.

Sometimes your clients will demand that you write a particular line of business. After enough requests you might decide to write that type of business. If you are a P&C agent on the commercial side, I would bet you have had many requests to write your clients' home and auto too.

Within commercial lines there is also a split between Property- Casualty and Workers' Compensation (technically a form of casualty insurance but by Property-Casualty I mean Commercial Property, Auto, General Liability, Inland Marine, Crime and Umbrella/Excess Liability). When California experienced a very hard Workers' Compensation market at the beginning of this century, my book had a high proportion of Work Comp business. This caused problems for my errors and omissions because some of the insurers were uneasy about insuring agencies with a large percentage of a particular line of insurance such as

Work Comp.

22777329R00094

Made in the USA
Lexington, KY
13 May 2013